Poetic Expression
Of
Teenage Depression

Poetry…

*To me, poetry has always been the most powerful form of expression.
It has helped me figure out the problems in my life, as well as myself,
piece by piece. It has taught me to look at life from more than just a single
perspective. It has helped me see the light in the darkest of times.
Most importantly, it has given me an outlet to channel my negative energy
into artwork, rather than keeping it bottled up inside,
or spreading it amongst others.*

*This book is a collection of poems that I wrote in high school.
They have been sitting in my room collecting dust for years.
This is my attempt to make something useful of them,
and hopefully inspire others to…*

*Create light from within,
When you can't find it outside.*

*To those lost in the dark,
May these poems bring you light.*

- Justin Allen Hester

Contents

The Lonely Moon
M.W.L.
Arachnophobia
A Dance With The Night
When The Planets Fall In Line
Is This Just A Dream?
Her Only Sin
The Lightning Strikes
Dirty Knees
Forgive And Forget
After Life
God Doesn't Need Donations
The Man Behind The Mask
Revenge
This Dark Night
Confessions
Escape
Please Stay
If Secrets Told Themselves
J.
Wish
Nothing But A Dream
As Midnight Falls
Off Liquor Drenched Lips
On Halloween
Fate Or Coincidence?
Two Minutes 'Till Midnight
The One That Will Last
Taken For Granted
Karma's Not A Bitch
A Heart So Shallow

The Lonely Moon

I'm slowly wandering the graveyard,
The only place where I feel wanted.
For these memories are trapped in me,
And now I'm cold and haunted.
These tombstones are my new friends,
Completely surrounding me.
Thousands of them, closing in,
Just like these haunted memories.

The lonely moon above is full,
And the stars are shining bright.
Reminds me when we'd gaze into them,
Conversing through the night.
I'd die to hear your voice again,
But thick silence fills the air.
Quickly broken by a distant cry,
I was shocked to see you there.

I ran your way and screamed your name,
But it's as if you didn't hear.
You sat there somberly on your knees,
Shedding mournful tears.
Your right hand held a rose,
And an empty bottle of wine.
In your left hand lay the note,
In which I asked you to be mine.

Now I stand here in confusion,
Because you won't look at me.
Then I noticed your eyes fixed on a tombstone,
Shadowed by a dying tree.
The clouds unblocked the moon light,
Then I slowly came to find…
The tombstone stealing your attention,
Just happened to be mine.

M.W.L.

*M*ystery lies within,
A riddle you won't comprehend.
Right before your clueless eyes,
The name I love, secretly lies,
Hidden in the words and lines.
And at no point will you ever find

*W*hat it is you're looking for.
Hope is really all you've got,
If you intend to solve the plot.
Three words that mean the most to me,
Nestled within, so simply.
Examine these words carefully,
Your name will appear so obviously.

*L*ook at every word and every line,
And in between these verses you'll find
Who this puzzle is all about.
However, don't search too hard
Or the name might not stand out.
Remind yourself, without a doubt.
Never, is when this love will end.

Arachnophobia

The spider kills the fly,
This life's a metaphor.
This web is wound so tight,
I can't move anymore.

The life of a fly
Is already much too brief,
Yet cut shorter by the spider,
And stolen like a thief.

So simple for the spider,
And deadly for the fly,
Unaware with just one step
That he's soon going to die.

The beauty of the web
And it's irresistible attraction,
Caused this unsuspecting fly
To be helplessly lured in.

Comforting at first,
His trust would weave within the web,
Unaware with just one step,
He would soon be dead.

My conception of the spider has changed so drastically,
Such a cold blooded killer, yet intellectually.
I respect it's technique, so uniquely clever,
Yet my hate for this creature will live on forever.

A Dance With The Night

An unexpected, regretted prize,
Unexpected with a gaze in her eyes.
My death was a short dance with the night,
The darkness within her shines so bright.

A single night of stupidity
Is the forever burn of insanity.
Everlasting truth has come to a halt,
But never before was it not my fault.
The meaning in words can overwhelm,
The depth in thought is like another realm.
Those two bloody fangs in the side of my neck,
Draining the life with a vampire effect.
One foot in the dark, one foot in the light,
One step away from eternal night.
Unaware of the torture which lie ahead,
Caused by contradicted words once said.

I gave you enough rope to hang yourself,
And I've never done that for anyone else.
You've given up now, and I can tell,
I'd just rather be with you than by myself.

A fire is only intense as you intend,
And can turn to ashes when you want it to end.
Except a thoughtful mind is fuel to the flame,
The more complex, the less it tames.

When The Planets Fall In Line

There are too many stars in the midnight sky,
Disappearing into space with the blink of an eye.

I've been searching for one that shines so bright,
That I can look up and find it anytime of the night.

Yet the clouds are too thick, fog is all that I see,
Laying in the grass, slipping in and out of a dream.

Is This Just A Dream?

I see faces in the shadows on my walls.
I watch them creep around me, and watch them crawl.
Moonlight shines through my window,
But it's too dim to kill them all.

I close my eyes and wonder,
Is this just a dream?
If this nightmare is reality,
Why are they haunting me?

I see spirits in the darkness behind my door,
As the door slowly opens, I see more.
The candle's lit beside me,
But it's not bright enough to cure.

I close my eyes and wonder,
Is this just a dream?
If this nightmare is reality,
Why are they haunting me?

I hear whispers taunting me from all around.
My hands cover my ears to escape the sound.
I peer into the night,
But they're nowhere to be found.

I close my eyes and wonder,
Is this just a dream?
If this nightmare is reality,
Why are they haunting me?

Her Only Sin

The walls surrounding me are the darkest shade of black,
I wish this wasn't happening, insomnia's coming back.
My mind is recreating the torture of that sinister sin,
As if the first time wasn't bad enough, it's happening again.
This reoccurring nightmare, as the sun begins to fall,
The memories get more vivid as darkness covers my walls.

I've been wondering why for quite some time,
I've been dying to find the reason behind…

Her only sin.

The Lightning Strikes

I've been waiting and anticipating this day for quite a while,
The sun forced down my back, your lips are forced to smile.

Then the lightning strikes,
What a tragic change of events.

As the sun fades slowly, so does the smile,
Mistaken sinful secrets, hidden with useless denial.

Then the lightning strikes,
What a tragic change of events.

The lightning has never burned so bright,
The thunder has never roared so loud,
Now the moon is partially hidden
Behind a wispy pair of clouds.

The sky's lit up completely, but only for a second,
Which is long enough to blind, and force this misconception.

Dirty Knees

No amount of apologies,
Or begging on your dirty knees,
Can get rid of these memories,
Or take back what you've done to me.

Forgive and Forget

A chill shoots down my back, straight through my spine,
That memory strikes me like lightning, that one sick line.
The room has never felt so cold, though I can barely feel at all.
How can everything change so drastically due to a single flaw?

Now I'm contemplating what to do,
Deciding if I should go through
With this, or is this just a big mistake?
Or is this what it'll have to take…

To forgive and forget.

I've never felt so in control,
For the first time it's my turn to glow.
For better or worse, I'll soon know
What lay ahead this blinding track
Of memories you can't take back.
And if the fairy tales you told were true,
Then Karma's coming after you.

Now I'm contemplating what to do,
Deciding if I should go through
With this, or is this just a big mistake?
Or is this what it'll have to take…

To forgive and forget.

Now there's so much power at my fingertips,
Growing with the thought of your selfish lips.
I could change lives with just one slip.
So the end as come, and here it goes,
The sins and secrets fly out the windows.
Now I stopped breathing, my heart stopped beating,
The light got so bright that I can't even see…

Then it all came back to me
As if I woke up from a dream,
Lying on the floor
With your picture next to me…

I've been let down once again,
I'll get used to your cold skin.
I give up on forgiving,
And I know I won't forget.

After Life

Curiosity,
Constantly questioning me,
Do I have something to look forward to,
Or is it just a dream?

Is it well worth it to worship?
Seems like just a waste of time,
Spending all your years anticipating death…
Well, what about your life?

God Doesn't Need Donations

I'm not falling for these fairy tales
You expect me to believe,
About a man who lives within the clouds
That nobody can see.
A man that you must worship
'Till you meet the reaper and his scythe,
Spending all your years anticipating death,
Well, what about your life?

God forbid you don't bow to him,
(Only his slaves are sent above)
You'll be sentenced to eternal torture…
Now is that what you call love?

The Man Behind The Mask

Constantly let down by the man behind the mask,
The constant drowning of the emptying flask,
Persuading him into forbidden attractions,
Following through with hypocritical actions.
The seven fingers of everlasting trust,
Overwhelmed by the seven fingers of lust.
Honesty and innocence are now traits of the past,
Alive one minute, but dead so fast.

Now he's hiding behind his mask of lies,
Concealing away his misleading eyes.
Understanding, regretfully, what's truly missed.
A belief in something which no longer exists.
His talent lies in his misconception,
Keeps you gazing in the wrong direction.
A newfound passion in a newfound sin,
A feeling of comfort in such a sweet revenge.

The room is dark,
But I know he's here.

I hear his breathing,
He has to be near.

I see his eyes,
Then I see him stare.

This candle is lit,
The figure is getting clearer…

The man behind the mask, is the man in the mirror.

Revenge

This one's for you, once again.
Yet you still won't comprehend.
After all these words, and all these lines,
And every second of wasted time,
It's your name that's getting old.
So here's a dish that's best served cold.
It happens to be my new favorite treat,
Never before has it been this sweet.

This Dark Night

I step outside to have a smoke,
The gray clouds fill the sky.
As I'm wondering where you are,
The sun's nowhere in sight.
A cold breeze blows as the crows swarm low,
To escape the rain on this dark night.

…This dark night.

I've been wishing on the stars,
But it never seems to make a difference.
Because I'm sitting alone as the fire burns slow,
On this dark night.

…This dark night.

If tonight wasn't such a nightmare,
I could escape this isolation.
But the mere thought of the happiness in your screams,
Brings me nothing except frustration.

To be a gentleman was what I've tried,
Now I'm spilling out these thoughts of mine.
Consider this my final goodbye,
For this is my last line.

Confessions

Hidden within these walls
Are the confessions I have made.

For someone, they would kill,
To another, they would save.

I'm concentrating on the words,
Which secrets hide behind…

Who I dream about at night.

Escape

I'm lost in the dark,
Searching for something I'll never find.
These woods close in around me,
This lake reflects the night.
To escape is what I strive for,
Yet I'm still not left alone.
This fire that burns inside me,
Can't even cure this cold.

Take a glance into the stars,
Lay with me beside the lake.
Take a glance into the stars,
Let me be your escape.

These stars shine bright above me,
Then I noticed now's the time.
You already made your wish,
Which contradicted mine.

Take a glance into the stars,
Lay with me beside the lake.
Take a glance into the stars,
Let me be your escape.

I'm taunted by the faces
Which lurk within the trees.
The shadows kill them off,
But it's your voice which rescues me.
It's the beauty of your voice,
Which kills these ugly memories.

Take a glance into the stars,
Lay with me beside the lake.
Take a glance into the stars,
You… are my escape.

Please Stay

Smile, sweet child,
Watching the stars makes it all worthwhile.

Sing, to the moon,
Only a fool would give up so soon.

Dance, down by the lake,
For this is your greatest mistake.

Listen, to the crows,
Telling secrets nobody else knows.

Stay, I'll pray,
That this moment never fades away.

If Secrets Told Themselves

If only you could understand,

Or if secrets told themselves,

I could find my way from this dark place,

You could save me from this hell.

J.

*J*ust you, is who I dream of,
W*e* both have true hearts.
Ju*s*t you seem to understand,
I've *s*een it from the start.
This *i*s my form of confession,
For se*c*rets are wrong to hide.
Search *a*round these words, it's your name which lies inside.

Wish

Another day comes to an end
With no one to call my own.

So tonight, I'll dream of you and me
As I lie in bed alone.

My eyes are closing slowly,
Reality's fading fast.

Finally, my wish comes true,
It's you and me at last.

Nothing But A Dream

Last night I dreamed a thousand dreams,
A thousand dreams of you and me,
But woke to find they're make believe.
You're nothing but a dream.

Tonight I'll dream a thousand dreams,
A thousand dreams of you and me,
But this time I will not believe
Unless I wake to see you here with me.

This morning I woke up all alone,
Alone inside this empty home,
So I guess I'll just go back to sleep,
And sleep for an eternity…
For you're nothing but a dream.

As Midnight Falls

Step by step, I make my way,
As the smoke clouds trail behind.
There's no destination in which I'm heading,
But it's you I always find.
I hear the echo of your voice,
It comes from deep inside.
There's no *escape* from this curse you've cast,
You're always on my mind.

As midnight falls, I stand alone.

Oh the things I'd sacrifice,
To see you here with me.
I take a glance around,
Yet there's only memories.
This all feels so familiar,
We were together here once before.
Oh the things I'd sacrifice,
To see you here once more.

As midnight falls, I stand alone.

Off Liquor Drenched Lips

I arrived to find you weeping in the shadows, all alone.
Then you threw your arms around my neck,
And your skin just felt so cold.

You confessed it all in whispers,
Which crept slowly into my ears.
Though it was only the consumption which revealed
The three words I've been dying to hear…

On Halloween

Let's take a walk into the darkness,
Where our secrets shine so bright.
Your costume is quite foolish,
Yet it's not fooling me tonight.

Take this crown of sorrow,
Rest it upon your thoughtless head,
For you've killed the better part of me,
And left me here for dead.

So, try your tricks,
Am I just your treat?

I'll get revenge,
Which is much more sweet.

Fate or Coincidence?

Oh, sweet memories,
Your happiness brings irony.

For you, I believe this must be sacred,
Yet it took so much to realize.

Is this fate or coincidence?
We danced with death, and both survived.

Two Minutes 'Till Midnight

Day after day, I lived a lonely lie,
'Till you came to break this curse,
For only a kiss from your sweet lips,
Could quench this awful thirst.

Despite my bittersweet sacrifice,
I conquered this wrongful lust.
Don't shed a tear, nor fear me dear,
For my heart is one you'll trust.

The sound of raindrops on my window,
The curtains drawn to block moonlight,
I'm wide awake as my dreams come true,
Two minutes 'till midnight.

The One That Will Last?

Now stricken with joy,
It's all but the best…
For the sadness and sorrow,
Has been put to rest.

To kill and to conquer,
What was destined by fate…
Living solely to find,
The "*one*", the "*escape.*"

Though I've tried and I've failed,
I've learned from my past…
Hoping for once,
You're the one that will last.

Taken For Granted

It's never enough to please, of course,
Always searching for better,
Yet finding the worst.

I had all I needed in the palm of my hand,
Briefly taken for granted,
Now alone, here, I stand.

Karma's Not A Bitch

I woke up this morning thinking about
All the things I forgot about,
Like how I've always been the bigger man,
Because I'd rather see you smile than pout.

The one thing you never realized,
I've always seen it in your eyes,
You can't just sit back, relax,
And expect everything to fall in line.

See, Karma's not a bitch…
You are.
I hate to break it to you.

I picked you a rose on your birthday,
I had no money to buy you anything,
But they say it's the thought that counts,
So why's it dying on my dresser?
I've been trying to figure that out.

Just because everything doesn't go your way, or make your day,
Doesn't mean that karma has to pay you back.

Just keep in mind, for every time you fucked me over…
Karma's gonna fuck you back.

See, Karma's not a bitch…
You are.

I hate to break it to you.

A Heart So Shallow

The rain falls slow from the black sky,
Now I've never known a heart so shallow.
I saw the lightning strike in the distance,
Yet the thunder never seemed to follow.

For every step which I've took forward,
They've all taken two steps back.
It's so hard to forget someone,
When their knife's still in your back.

Now everything which I hold sacred,
Rests so softly within these hands.
All these years spent comprehending,
It's the only thing I seem to understand.

I found a way to clear these rainclouds,
Now I see the moon tonight.
When you spend so much time in the darkness,
It's so hard to find your way back to light…

www.ingramcontent.com/pod-product-compliance
Lightning Source LLC
Chambersburg PA
CBHW031513210526
45464CB00007B/2890